House of Affection

House of Affection

poems by
Wendy Wood Kwitny

The Sheep Meadow Press
Riverdale-on-Hudson, New York

All inquiries and permission requests should be addressed to:

> The Sheep Meadow Press
> 5247 Independence Avenue
> Riverdale-on-Hudson, New York 10471

Distributed by the University Press of New England.
Designed and typeset by the Sheep Meadow Press.

Printed on acid-free paper in the United States. This book meets the guidelines for permanence and durability of the Committee on Production Guidelines for Book Longevity of the Council on Library Resources.

Library of Congress Cataloguing-in-Publication Data

Kwitny, Wendy Wood, 1957–
  House of affection / by Wendy Wood Kwitny.
        p. cm.
  ISBN 1-931357-14-5 (alk. paper)
  I. Title.
PS3611.W589H68 2004
811'.6--dc22

                                                        2004001990

We are grateful to the New York State Council on the Arts, a state agency, for their support.

Acknowledgments
Alabama Literary Review, "Evening's Chair"
Mudfish 10, "Bachelor Room"

for Woody and Peter

Table of Contents

One

Two

Now I know what I am and what I was
I know the distance that runs from a man to the truth
I know the word the dead love best

from Vicente Huidobro, *The Return Passage*

One

I turn my head or hide it in my blouse.
I have a window without a house.
It still opens and shuts.
I put a handle on it and carry it like a cage.
At times I scribble the word "door,"
but there's no getting in
or out.

House of Affection

When you live on a mountain,
you begin to identify with your cliff,
and rise above the usual concerns,
as if the reasons for sadness
would become exhausted
before they got to you.

I was wrong and now the living room
belongs to someone else.
The room where I announced both pregnancies.
The step where his foot first faltered.
From below, I heard him fall
and yelled, Are you okay?
He said he was, but in four months,
he was gone.

Morning light pushes the final darkness
behind a cabinet.
Named Casa Cariños, or House of Affection,
made of wood and glass,
our house made room
for every bird, tree, and child,
it was as if the mountain lived inside.

I barely recall how the rest of it was lost:
the painting of a man sitting at a piano,
a worn, red velvet chair,
an Italian dog warning sign
that could tell you nothing about
our dogs, Henry and Edgar,
now in the company of others,
and the fallen giant of a sofa
where all of us sat.

Six years ago my husband put on a tux
and hiking boots in that lower room,
I, a long dress and Wellingtons;
we walked out to a muddy clearing
and said we would,

while a hundred rained-on people stood
and watched; sunlight soon
lowered the sails of black umbrellas
and the damp sky
brought out every kind of blue.

On the mountain where the local boys
once collected arrowheads;
in the downstairs room,
that had not been a nursery for long,
among small pieces of mint green furniture,
soft yellow elephants, and a suspended
mobile of unblinking clowns,
to part with you,
I put on a black dress and plain shoes.

We had no idea how soon,
after a simple stumble on a step,
the truth we learned
concerning love and each other
would stop like a book,
be of no further use,
like umbrellas in a dry place.

A little over a year later,
the children and I are residents on a town street,
with old trees carefully in a row;
our small gray house has fewer windows,
but also fewer places to fall.
Our chipmunk
is now the suburban squirrel,
making a dog long to be off its leash.
Here, my boys and I build mountains
out of blocks or stones or mud,
but mostly out of love.

As for today,
snow has kept everybody home,
every house, car, and tree
is turned white and glittery.
The mood is light-hearted, Alpine.
Bundled neighbors bend over shovels

like little people from children's books
while the round, red-faced children
are like flowers in the snow.
It should seem more cold
beyond this table of abandoned cereal bowls,
the flickering TV,
and the toy trains that rrrrh away
in perpetual stillness.

I rise from our bed alone.
The house was turned
into an object to sell,
an inventory of words
like a collection of stones
rubbed into certain points
like tiny grave markers.
The trees were returned to paper
and our mountain folded up.
My heart, like the orange salamander,
comes out only when it rains.

Not every hour longs for a phrase.
Not every room needs a sofa,
or every person, another person,
or every child, his father,
but of course,
those are white lies.
One day the snow will melt.
Perhaps I will know then
where I put the paintings, the dog sign,
and all the rest of our things,
why you never climb out of my head
and be the way you were when you were anything
but a collection of words.

Piano

I want to go home
said the small, blond boy at the door
of his house and I knew
what he meant, how the heart
has a different number and street
and its door opens perpetually to a man
we cannot find in these rooms,
these real rooms I have painted the color
of flowers longing for this interior winter,
this winter of the heart to end,
these beautiful rooms and halls
a widow and her two small boys wander
not knowing what else to do
like a certain length of music
in search of a piano.

January 20, 2000

Out of the sighs of a morning you never really noticed
such as the hundreds of geese gathered at the road
like spectators watching your car pass,
the redness of your hands as they steered you toward
another failed moment,
and above them, a blank, January sky,
or what you thought about at the traffic light.

Was it only the past that suddenly mattered?
How magically your children grew in the back seat,
out of the roof and rear windows,
when you closed your eyes for a minute.
Oh tell me that every word said and not said
would have meant more
if I could only remove this tower of hats

I've borrowed from the world,
and stop backing out, and driving away.

Ordinary Time

Mornings I would nurse the baby
in the backseat of a cab on the way to the hospital;
darling he, bewildered I, both strangers
in the world we rode by.

Past kiosks and shop windows
selling their variation of every fifteenth
minute: a breath mint, a hairdo,
a popular actor, a pointed shoe;
past people walking and talking
while they raced in all directions,
past restaurants of ravenous people
raising cups and lowering spoons,
noting the time and pointing here, there,
an air of self-importance everywhere!
Invisible clocks ticking and tocking
as day turned to night and night, day.
The same busy people on Saturdays and Sundays
rushing to museums and to brunch,
hurrying on little wheels racing here, there,
or just jogging until they disappeared,
everyone running from life or death?

Breathless, I stared,
certain their definition of beauty
was not a thin man in a backless gown.
I wondered if I would ever find the hole
to climb back into that world again,
if indeed, I should ever want to.
At the hospital, I would hand my sleeping baby
over to the sitter and vanish into an elevator
where time wasn't ordinary at all.
As the elevator stopped forever on every floor,
I refused to tell time a thing.
At last in my husband's room,
with love covering the numbers on the clock's face,
I would curl up next to him on the bed,
and for awhile, we would pretend to care,
what was for lunch or whether it would rain.

The Uncountable Tears of the World

Auden often walked with me
in the halls, repeating
They are and suffer, that is all they do,
or About suffering they were never wrong
the Old Masters.

And a boy would fall from the sky,
and I would watch in horror,
as the older poet nudged me in the room.

It never mattered to his lines
that I did not exist.

They all came,
all the poets with all their words
stringing lights, like paper lanterns
in a darkness that preferred
a monogram.

As every word became
so crucial, a weary Eliot would insist
That is not what I meant
That is not what I meant at all

and having no trousers to roll up
or beach to wander,
my husband would gaze out the window
for uncustomary hours in a silence so personal
my eyes would sting

In the lower room, in solitude,
I put on a white dress and combed my hair
to go to the hill to marry you.

In the lower room, in solitude,
I put on a black dress and combed my hair
to go to the hill to bury you.

In solitude, in another room,
I sit on a chair, away from the hill,
combing the night for the rest of you.

Planet Cancer

Planet Cancer
has its own language,
laws, and answers.

In hospital, inhospitable,
for instance,
no less a little Egypt
where surgeon gods
and doctor kings
stroll among
the tubing trees.
At the pyramid top
there is barely room
for the giant heads,
who listen to hearts
they cannot hear.

Ranked below them
whirl the worker bees
of busy nurses,
undoing and redoing
almost everything,
and the smiling women
with clipboards pressed
against their business-suited breasts,
armored to do their best
to be sensitive and kind,
for much went in
to training them;
and then the men with brooms
who sweep and bleach
the germy rooms.

Lower than the staff,
the next of kin are next
to last,
mulattos in a sense,
for none are sick
and none are well,

as if the idea of death
could be caught like a cold,
neighbors bid them hello
from afar;
to the doctors,
they are little more than slaves,
naked and dull-minded,
told to go away
or come back
or do this or do that
or stand in the hall.

But lower than all,
no matter what they did
in real life,
are those who now
must live patiently,
their identity left at home
with the rest of their things;
depending on people
they have never met,
who glide with ease
around the borrowed beds;
their children viewed
largely from photographs;
as for their dignity,
how many cups can one fill
before it goes?

The drugstore watch,
the florist rose,
the donated paperback,
all signs that they have disappeared.
Each suffers, frightened,
and barely alive;
emasculated men
and bony women
and children
without hair:
to swallow jello
is triumph here.

Planet Cancer
has the slowest elevator.
The doors close
like the jaws of a dull whale.
Everybody is swallowed up,
then spat out.

Quatrains

I drag my knowledge of death
round and round,
like a dog inside a house
with a bone to bury.

Sometimes I hate poetry.
Its attempt to box the heart
like the summer begonia
that dies as I write.

If I cannot pull these words
off my skin
like some sentimental tattoo,
you may dismiss me.

Nevertheless, this is the picture
my dots made.
I am not depressed.
Everybody else is in denial.

September 4, 2000

Death should be enough.
The cicadas remind me constantly.
Their hollowed selves hang
like little coats on walls and doors
while the rest sing like Greeks
longing to announce another tragedy.

Death should be enough in a small town.
Even a common death.
But most of us need to fit in such places.
I am like those animals that need leaves
from the highest trees, but find myself
so often among clouds.

I should like to speak of death
the way others do about today's rain or other weather,
unlatch the brackets of this endless clause,
but death is mostly for the novels now.
No one in New Jersey knows what to do with it.
We widows look like everybody else.

I have worn the sweaters of this town,
a weary creature pausing on a weary leaf
or like a nun without a habit.
Bronze Eros sleeps and sleeps;
in the houses the husbands come and go.
My sons read books about the dinosaurs.

To press my face against the body I loved,
not my hand across his name –
now a blank on every form,
a phantom leg or phantom arm.
The clouds have overtaken the upper rooms.
Mercifully, my children sing louder than the bugs.

You are suddenly pushed
into a theater, handed a black dress,
and told to grieve.

They pause, waiting for you to cry.
But you hoard tears,
bringing them only out at night.

Nothing hides the nakedness.
Not the dress, the coat, or hat.
You insist they put the other part back,

and lay your body across the bed
like a hat or a coat
in a dress that is black.

For Susanna

1

When a man begins to die
and he is your husband,
the memory of his strength
belies the new reality:

a man confined to a hospital bed,
a few family photos temporarily
imposed on the room's framed prints
of bridges and flowers.

But as his wife, he has led you
backstage to see how he breaks,
what terrifies him, and has shown
you his secret collection of tears.

When a man begins to die
and he is your father,
you are completely unprepared.
The new reality confounds the former view,

the one you took from a velvet seat
as the curtain parted;
no matter how many times he entered,
you never once saw him cry.

Unprepared for such a man
to grow so thin,
the rest of the world
fractures beneath you

but in such fine, hairline cracks
you do not notice the ground is gone
until the day the world has finally failed to notice
how wonderful you are.

2

She was in the backseat of the car,
a young woman sleeping like a child,

as her god drove on a dark night in a snowstorm
across endless Pennsylvania.

I sat with her father in the front,
bracing myself, wide awake,
knowing I was with a man
who was also worried.

Occasionally he would reach over
to press my knee in reassurance.
It felt as if we would never arrive.
As she stumbled drowsily from the car, up the stairs

to bed, her dreams practically undisturbed,
he went to the liquor cabinet and poured a drink.
We arrived, and we keep arriving
at a desired moment we can never keep.

Hop on Pop

> We like to hop
> We like to hop
> On top of Pop
> — Dr. Seuss

for Mark Malone

I needed at least one giant
for the boys to crawl over,
who would shake them off,
rising up
to toss them in the air
or twirl them in a circle,
whirring like an airplane.

A giant
who could stoop low enough
to meet them eye to eye.

One who resembled their father,
and would growl with them,
or read to them in a lower voice,
who could point out the world
as one boy rides his shoulders
and the other holds his hand,
or would stand with them in the grass
to hurl an infinite variety
of rounded objects into the sky,
noting how each one spins and descends,
as each boy leaps, thrilled at the catch.

As a woman,
I am a fairly good dad,
but it would never occur to me
that a handle off a plastic bucket
makes an enviable weapon;
that dangling straps from a backpack shoot;
that watching backhoes and front loaders

might be interesting live or on video;
that the ugliest Batman pajamas
are what my boys, neither one standing
any taller than thirty-seven inches,
prefer to a print of Swedish reindeer;
for I am finally not a man,
no matter how strong I am or capable I feel.

But a man attended my husband's funeral
and in the mystery of his promise
to a man already dead, his friend,
has laid himself down to show the boys
how wonderful it is to be exactly as they are;
while he is here,
both fight to wear his hat
or curl up beside him,
making themselves as small as kittens
as the giant's great, hairy hands
stroke their soft, sweet heads.

When Winter Began

In his absence, I have found only absence,
not even an inferior him.

I try to reconstruct my husband with words.
Instead, I make a man of words.

Death has pulled away all interferences of the night,
making me an ancient who knows too much about the stars,

how sorrow was put into the sky,
why a dry tear is less real than one that falls.

I have become so acquainted with darkness,
my eyes adjust like an owl's,

but my desire to go on
is like the nocturnal bird's blackened flight.

I want to hold or behold my husband. Instead,
I string letters round and round the moment winter began.

I fill a chair with tears, and then a room, and close the door
so that the children won't hear.

Beyond the Trees

In the barn,
your name was everywhere,
yellowing in cartons and on shelves;
love letters
from every woman who ever loved you,
were waiting, it seemed,
for the day you would not return.

I met all your different selves
that made me love you again and again,
and sometimes hate you.

For hours I would read,
deciding which pages were worth keeping,
making leaning towers
of all the appropriate categories.

This was before the stone was carved.
After such a day,
I would go to the vague spot in the cemetery
longing to lay my body across your grass.

Instead I would just stand there,
staring at our mountain
beyond the trees,
trying to reconcile your vacancy
with mine.

Synecdoche

Even a plain white mug
can bring him back.

A mindless act:
reaching for something
to put coffee in.
I remember when he bought it,
just one, because it reminded him
of mornings with his parents.

How many mornings with him
passed uneventfully,
with no need to notice a plain cup.
It was enough
that he stood in the kitchen
using one.

But to relive an early one in Orvieto
when he went to bring me cappuccino
and returned so happy
to tell me how lively the cafes
were at that hour,
to imagine a simpler way of life,
where time seems more abundant,
more beautifully made –

or the Roman waiter
who a few days earlier,
had written his telephone number
in chocolate powder
on the milk foam of my coffee
and winked as he served it,
even though my husband sat across from me.
The gesture was too Fellini-like for any husband
to be upset with and mine laughed as he grabbed me outside
the restaurant, delighted I was his.

In poetry, a part used for a whole
makes an interesting device.
As for life, if only a plain white cup
could replace a man.

The Spirituality of Things

I found people
who could use
his sweaters.

Gave away all but two
of the Italian neckties
he had just bought
for his new job.

After making
a donation of his suits
to a local church,
I soon looked for them
in its basement,
wanting to touch them again,
to inform the person
buying them
of their provenance.

No one looking at it
could possibly guess
the value of the thirty-five dollar watch
bought to wear in the hospital,
that I put in my pocket
after his wrist stopped.

Archived in an old trunk
we bought for other things,
now a domestic coffin
that holds his letters and papers,
the blue shirt he wore the first night we met,
the one I wore the last,
with the television topping it
like a large black hat,
no one could guess what is enclosed.

How naturally we forget
the spirituality of certain things,

since most objects just sit on our shelves
waiting to be used.

Because there had been nothing
particularly special about them before,
it was the pair of trousers I changed into this evening
to take the children for a walk,
I had worn that night.

Unreal Estate

They would negotiate
the rocks, and call it business
as they offered me
much less.

They have tried to reduce this place
where we married on the hill
to so many square feet of closet space,
tile grout, and plumbing.

Rooms that held four years of our thoughts
and conversations and gave us rest
after climbing the mountain just out the door,
or all the mountains of metaphor, they called too small.

The trees were too tall, the river too cold;
I didn't even attempt to explain the emu pen.
Despite the babies needing changing on the rug,
they sniffed, and said it lacked a family room.

They would have me believe this house
means nothing beyond a sum of money and a deal.
For them it was quite clear,
the word widow pointed to a steal.

Ice cream

The houses are tidy in this town.
Every stoop holds a flowerpot.
People I will never know, nod hello.

I do not look unusual here,
where even the rain appears to fall
in straight, certain lines.

Still, I wonder if we belong.
Like a Saturday Evening Post cover
upon which is imposed

Munch's Scream,
mouth open without a sound,
recalling the flowers the nurses threw away.

In America,
where the pursuit of happiness
seems foremost, sorrow
is difficult to pull off.

For months I could still hear his car
crunching on the gravel
as he returned home from work,
see the baby toddle with both arms out
toward the front door repeating his first word.

Now when a stranger asks, What does your husband
do? I attempt to play down the Russian novel
I have dragged onto the playground,
and stands like an elephant beside me.

Like the others, she is usually unprepared
and kindly offers sympathy.
I don't want it.
I have two boys in the sandbox.

October 27, 2000

I want-,
       I want-,
             I want-

The sounds of my heart are an animal's
muffled under every hello and how are you.
But I will not complain of sadness,
only speak of it.

To transport the pleasure of this morning,
the sweetness of my children talking in their sleep,
the warmth of their tiny bodies claiming me like a tune,
a mug of coffee in a slightly cool room –

Our house is made of words and silences.
The way he put us together by name,
saying love first, I love you,
then withdrew, like a man off to a train.

The boxed geranium would belie this.
But only for awhile,
for sadness is more like the hemlock,
the tree that stood on all sides of our old house.

Here, the three of us long to call every word
for dad, attaching sticky mys to each,
instead we chant like the baby:

       I want-,
             I want-,
                   I want-
eyeing nothing in particular.
Our hearts beat like the wings of birds.

The first boy wants to climb into his father's photograph
and get him, he said.
Yesterday I tried to fall into one, a hopeless Alice,
hunting for the texture and feel of my husband's skin,
the familiar smell, wanting his arms to wrap
around me, the sound of his voice
to be more than memory.

Poem

If I burn this paper
and remember the words
the poem would not be lost,
so I think of fire,
of the passion that was buried
when they put the statue
that resembled my husband
into the ground,
but like these words
that are burned into my heart,
that are from my heart,
he cannot entirely be taken away.
Because he was just a man
when we first met,
just as this page is nothing more than paper,
but love gave him a name.
Returning home after a week away
I went to make the children's bed,
pulling back the covers I found
Michael, the boys' stuffed cat
and it made me smile,
and think, Hello, Michael.
In a room with at least fifty other
stuffed animals, this one had
a name because he was favored,
chosen over all the others
as I chose a man named Jonathan
to love and to be my husband
so no amount of dying
can kill him.
I am not a wizard with a phoenix
but a woman with little boys
who ask in the darkness of morning,
Has the sun come up yet?
This book is not a box of ashes,
or a fallen tree,
but handfuls of blackened words
collected to hold a man
for as many hours

as I can number,
not to entertain you,
but because the breath
that escapes
between my lips
seeks his
and falls instead like rain
on my children's faces and fingers,
or lingers on the door's pane.

Near Haiku

I would say more, but
I mourn too many deaths:
husband, lover, father,

wife

An Ordinary Day

In the parks
of mothers and children,
the occasional father
who silently pushes a child on a swing,
the brightness of the day generously
riddled under the trees,
who could know how each of them
might suffer, as a marriage becomes difficult,
a woman discontent, a man begins to doubt
whatever it was he once dreamed.
No one would expect, for instance, the person
playing a circle game with her two little boys,
a few months earlier,
lay her head upon her husband's chest
and heard the ending of his heart.
Carried by that silence
on a boat of disbelief and sorrow
along a river, so bottomless and dark,
away from the day when she was merely upset
that he did not want to come with them to the park,
for a reason she no longer remembers
and no longer matters.
She has learned to sing what the children like
and falls down gently
as they launch their tiny, new, imperfect words
into the blue of what seems
an ordinary day.

Woody and Peter

From the road at night
looking up,
our house glimmered through the trees
forming another constellation
we called Woody and Peter.

Beautiful stars,
how long we wished for them.

Giving them the names of our fathers
and our grandparents,
alluding to your beloved folksingers
and my saints, to the boy who teaches Wendy to fly,
taking the imagery of wood and rock,
we wanted to make them stronger
than us.

Almost a year has passed.
Woody sings through the alphabet,
and Peter, who had not even sat up
before you were gone,
now wobbles across the room like a lovable king.

Darling know,
after my ear heard your heart stop,
their milky light has steered me
through this long night
of your absence.

The Opening

I return to the day
you lost the rest of night
and every major and minor thing
such as the pleasure
of hearing your last child call for you,
for it would take two years
of naming ducks and dogs
before he realized
his word for dad
was as transient as a snowflake,
dissolving the instant
it fell upon someone warm,
forming instead
a place of longing in the heart,
as his brother's would

                                 if only

you could have taken Woody
just once to school as he proudly swings
his lunch box, or dribbles a ball,
or spells his name,
instead he turns from the window
to ask me now, why you cannot come
and what was your name,

                                 how long

can boys
believe in a superhero
who tried to fight a monster
called cancer, as I have told them
recently about you,
and not become as sad
as their mother

                                 how

every evening since that night
that went on without you,
the sight of a full moon,
or the silhouette of a winter tree,
becomes neither moon nor tree
but a reminder of your death,
and this new loneliness

like snow shoved into colossal drifts along the roadside,
or in our house the afternoon the doctor called,
making the other,
when you merely failed to understand me
so minor I would not notice it now;

is the blackened tree
the doorway or the moon behind it
the opening, my darling,

the boys are calling me,
carrying me away from this silence
I am trying to write my way out of.

One Mourning

Grief is as personal as a fingerprint.
A normal day, a matter of reprieve.

Anger might be the natural response,
but I am too tired for that.

Watch the endless combinations
of passers-by on a city street corner;

how many people for how many years
converge then split,

their brief solidarity resonating forever
unremarkably.

Tomorrow

When you know there is no reversing
the final verdict, the doctors are sorry,
there is nothing they can do,
death belongs to death.

Because no one can predict the very hour,
you wait, not knowing
which will be the last thing
you say, if it will happen
while you go
to get a coffee or feed the baby
or make a phone call.

For a day and a half I waited in dread.
The children were allowed and stayed for hours.
Everybody came to say goodbye, then left,
as nurses threaded in and out of the room
to adjust the morphine bag or to do
and undo the web of tubes,
another afternoon passed.

Close to midnight
we kissed and I withdrew
toward the door.
I had the younger child and needed rest,
for it could be days yet.
In four hours, I would return,
but after four months,
we were used to dying and to last words.
His gaze was different that night,
less brave, widening and so blue
as if to pull all of me in and memorize me,
faced with a part of the sky
I would never see again, I nodded,
repeating tomorrow, tomorrow,
I will see you tomorrow.
All through the next day,
I no longer knew what to say
or promise,

worried that the absence of a word
would make this delicate world
something worse.
Although he had never awakened,
I mentioned the rain had stopped,
and mentioned it again,
until I could think of nothing more
to say about clouds,
and the awful silence rowed in.

To my own dismay,
I became weary of dying;
boredom
took the place of last things.
I began flipping the pages of a magazine,
despising every banality, every
picture of a world that never existed,
and now existed less,
wanting to build a cathedral instead,
and yet I devoured them, starved
for not just a lightness,
but an oblivion of being.

I would look up,
lost in a new blur of I love yous,
none of which he could return,
and lay my dull face across his gray hand,
still hunting for better words.
Now I long to take back that day.
I have so much more to say.

Thanksgiving Night, 1998

The last breaths are horrifying.
Furious for more life,
making us desperate
before a series of last things,
of seconds we wanted to chop in half,
and in half, and in half,
so that he wouldn't end.

And then he was gone.
No matter what I said.
And the clock continued
its ticky tocky,
and the nurses kept busy
with thisy and thaty,
doesn't anybody notice
my husband is dead,
the hand I hold is cold and black;
one nurse turns to pull off
his wedding band.

Wearing two,
I find the edge of the world
and fall off,
declaring
it is no longer round.

To call a hearse,
please deposit three dollars and fifty cents,
everything I touch
seems cold and black.
You have ten minutes
to speak to the artificial flower
who awakens at this hour
to assure me
he knows just what to do.

Outside, the city carries on
like a nervous dog, sniffing
every trash can and lamp post.

I wanted to say
something important had just occurred,
to go slower, be kind.

In Spite

In the event it will never matter
whether my husband, my children, or I
ever existed,

that the four of us may have been nothing more
than a certain, inconsequential grouping
of molecules,

no more important than dust,
that there will come a day when nobody will be left
to remember us exactly as we were,

that in spite of this, to have been here briefly
and loved them in such a vast way that made the universe
seem no bigger than a ceiling of glow-in-the-dark stars,

to have spent a single hour with any three of them
has been more astounding to me than the idea
of an infinite number of galaxies,

it has meant the world.

This sadness will not be finished,
but when I put a child under each arm,
there is a pause.

Today, watching the little one eat a plum,
while the two year old sat on the dog dish
claiming it for his relief,

I thought I would never stop laughing.

November 26, 2000

I would take back every harsh word,
and the angriest,
for one is too many
and none mattered,
as I measure each one now
against this silence.

My power to destroy you
was more devastating
than cancer,
for you loved me.
But I loved you too.
And you were a man
who needed me.

Two years ago today
you would have shown
angels the window,
if you could have,
and drawn the shade,
preferring to go to heaven
on an unmade bed

Two

The birth of Peter in June, the death of Jon in November. Lost between the first breath of my second child and his father's last, I roam a continent now with sheets upon almost every mirror. I have become like the eye that is absent from what it sees. Ultimately, I betray whatever group I sit among: the shadow of my widowhood lingering behind my chair in the rooms of mothers with small children; the light from my children dancing around me as I sit in the darker rooms with elderly widows. Although I cannot find my face, my heart is unequivocally defined, like the first bird that sings out the darkness of every early April morning, her flight hinged on the song's end. Parenthesized, like the curves of the Tao, facing each other, but here pulled apart, their opposite companionship like hands locked in a game of London Bridges, keeping this new language, these newly blackened words, from falling like a winged boy – or a flying girl still in her nightgown – until I am ready. Ready for what. The museums? The movies? The writing of sentences that will sentence me like everybody else to death? The blacknesses: waning in my emerging son seconds before oxygen called to his tiny lungs and turned him pink; waxing in my husband, as his heart weakened and blood departed, overtaking his fingers, hands, and feet like the ominous shadow of an object you cannot identify and will not stop; and now these words, like birds that name the sky by flying. Icarus falls into the sea, but Wendy survives, kept in a little house until she awakens. It's Peter's kiss that saves her, worn over her heart. It is out of this, when perhaps I am standing in the park pushing one of the boys on a swing or sitting at the sandbox watching both of them dig and pour, when no one has mentioned death, that I turn away and think of it like a row of boxwoods, neatly hedged so that I can look beyond at beautiful life. It is then I would like to shout from my heart something truthful, as I did in the hospital after Jon had lost his hair and so much weight and the doctors and nurses regarded him as little more than a point upon which to count blood cells and finish counting, not as the man who went with me to Block Island and made Peter. But I remain quiet or make a polite inquiry to another mother, like a bird that names the sky by flying.

True stories often long for some fiction. A happy ending. The dead cowboy who rises for a smoke. Better yet: the horse that rises from the smoke. True stories are not constructed, but tumble out of an ordinary morning, from a cup of coffee to a telephone call to opening the mail to a nap for the children, a moment in the garden for their parents, and just before noon, just as lunch was being put on the plates, what appears to be a stroke for the husband. But since he has just made love to you outside on such a beautiful summer morning, and you are already making plans for August, and my God, you just had the baby! Three weeks old, following the first boy by just sixteen months. A new job for him. The house up for sale. The smell of basil. How could your husband's leg just stop having any feeling? In a few more hours, when you are seated at your husband's desk, after you returned home from the hospital with the children, though he is still there, because you have no idea that this is a tragedy, the first steps toward an inconsolable ending, you think it is a precursor stroke, no permanent damage, a warning, diet modification, that sort of thing – the doctor calls and says the stroke was caused by a bleeding brain tumor. Nodules were also found in the lungs and liver. You say, because up to this point everything in your life did have some fiction attached to it, some residue of a dream, you say to the doctor, so how are you going to fix it. And he says he can't. Suddenly the old world, the world you at least were familiar with for the past forty-one years has crumbled in your lap. And with it, all of its fictions. I was tempted to write instead: And with it, all of its fictions. Then the baby cried. But neither child cried. Both were with me but I remember only the silence, vast amounts of it. As if it were suddenly winter and the roof had been pulled away and snow had fallen into the house and covered the floors and drifted against the walls.

You have been dropped from the sky. Like Wendy, the lost boys find you, you who are also lost. They wonder what type of house you would like, for they shall build one around you, walls raised to protect a fallen self, a wearied self. The British call a small house or playhouse a Wendy house, a place of pretend. In Arabic, the word for a verse of poetry is called house. We moved to a house on a mountain called Casa Cariños, or House of Affection. There are no tears in the house of poetry, said Sappho. But there are tears here, falling like rain on the dry flowers between these lines, just as there were tears in the house on the mountain. In the end is my beginning, wrote Eliot. In the beginning was the Word, said God. That is why I rise in darkness hours before the children call my name. To reconstruct the flight of the arrow that shot Wendy, from her heart as she lay on the ground to the moment in the sky when life and death danced with such velocity a hundred sheets of blank white paper wept. Like the roses the lost boys made-believe to grow up the walls of the sleeping girl's house, I make-believe a hundred paper bridges that bend from him to now.

A friend once said in an essay that for him narrative was little more than gossip, it was just a matter of degree. But these pages require more words: how many words to satisfy the portrait of a fifty-seven year old man, his forty-one year old wife, their two children, and all the lives we lived that brought us to that moment on the mountain when Jon would collapse forever. As I unpack a carton of books today, his books, each one seems to point to a future, no matter how historical, because they were collected and wait to be revisited. To handle each one now, put aside a few to read later, to note their physical presence alone: the weight and feel and smell of them, is to see his hand, reaching for one from the shelf, and watch him settle in a chair; to know he will never have their pleasure again. "The best ways to reconstruct a man's thinking is to rebuild his library..." observed Marguerite Yourcenar in her notes for Hadrian's Memoirs. Instead of a mausoleum: a library, or at least, an extra room set aside for just his books; there, the boys can wander among the titles and meet him at least part of the way. Like anybody's death, this will never make sense, because he has ended, the way a book ends: a man's whole life contained between two dates, 23 March 1941 to 26 November 1998, a pair of days like the pair of marble lion bookends I place on the shelf. Only his name and his written words remain in the world. And no matter how many words I write about him, none can be the faint smell of bay rum on his face in the morning after he's shaved or the sight of him walking with the dogs down the path or the sound of him singing in the shower and playing a cowboy song on the guitar to the baby or the slight bittery taste of bourbon on his lips at the end of the day; I cannot write the arm that used to pull me closer to him. From jacket and tie, to dust jacket, to a dust jacket covered in dust, from dust to dust, ashes to ashes, ashes, ashes we all fall down.

19 July. The morning following the day he collapsed, you awaken with an image of your husband floating out to sea on a black inner tube. It seems almost an absurd image, yet you can still remember the faded blue of the sky and water, as he turned away. Precisely one year later, driving away from his grave, you notice a cart stacked with black inner tubes at a gas station. This: an object you have not noticed since childhood, have not noticed that whole year, and have not seen since. A few months later, the tombstone you had carved in the stone yard at St. John the Divine is finished. Since it has been made by an artist who took the commission mostly out of sympathy, you arrange to transport it yourself to the country. He packs it into the back of your stationwagon. The children are in their car seats, a babysitter sits in the front with you. Although you hardly know her, she now lives with you, employed for the Princeton house for no other reason than fear. Fear that should anything happen to you, someone would be with the children. You rarely speak to each other, not out of animus, but for a lack of anything to say. She is from the West Indies and her beautiful face seems to have his shadow across it. She is as dark as he was fair; her nearly relentless silence, making room for everything he ever said to you; her slower movements now in place of his; she has become an embodiment of your loss, a persistent reminder that you have stepped into a completely different world, overshadowed by an enormous past that broke into so many pieces that you cannot put it back together. After you deliver the stone to the funeral home, you go to a diner for lunch. Facing each other, smiling politely when you catch each other's eyes, you long for an empty place to rest your gaze. You happen to look down at your wedding ring and notice it has broken. When you remove it to examine it closer, it breaks in half. I look up. Mirrored in the shock and disbelief of her large, round black eyes, you vanish like a small plane.

After talking to the doctor on the telephone, you call Margaret who lives two miles away. She and her husband are British and instead of carrying a large boat over a mountain as the hero did in the movie, Fitzcarraldo, they moved a whole, one-room schoolhouse to the spot next door where their garage had been, which they also moved, one board at a time. You tell her there is an emergency, would she drive you to the hospital immediately. She is used to rescuing you. Up until your first baby, you and your husband were Emerson and Thoreau on the mountain: you learned how to build a fire, find dry kindling from snow-covered woods, pull a dead duck out of the wood stove, cross-country ski straight out the front door, raise golden pheasant chicks every spring, and pick enough morels out the back door to make a stew once a year. During the summer, at the end of the day, your husband would fill a mason jar with martinis and take it down to the river to swim with the beavers. In the past when he had to travel for the book, you let the dogs sleep on the bed and never worried. But the mountain was too treacherous to be alone with a newborn baby. When I brought Woody home from the hospital, a February storm had just left the mountain so icy, Jon had to strategize how to get both of us up the last hill; he had me strap on ice cleats for one. So Margaret was used to spending the night with me or bringing me supplies. Once, during a blizzard, she grabbed a volunteer rescue worker from the new fire station next door (where the old schoolhouse had been), and brought him up. It was a good thing, for as soon as I closed the door to leave with them, the power went. Once settled in the back seat of the car, Woody, probably no older than a month, bundled with only a crescent of his small face showing, drew on his pacifier as he watched me, his small round eyes burning in the whitened night with absolute love and trust. When it snowed on the mountain, it was Russia; when the wind blew, it was the Old Testament; if it was a very rainy summer, mosquitoes dined on us. The only thing we didn't fear was the Flood. When she came for you that afternoon to take you back to the hospital, she said she would never forget the look on your face when she swung open the front door: horror.

Doing the dishes awhile ago I looked out the window to see snow falling on the daffodils. It was as if all those yellows had barely clawed their way out of the colorless ends of winter with its still pale sky and pointy twigs, to be mocked or belied by the sudden erasure. Winter, having no regard for what such a flower means to us, continued her untamed course. Instead of four seasons, it's more like eight, as each overlaps, waiting to overcome the next. The text would prefer that the snow be deleted from the daffodils. It yearns for the clarity and order of the novel, of the seasons, of any other attempt to make less delicate the vanishing hooves of time and experience. I too should like to tell you with the coming of the daffodils, that Jon's tumors were resolved, that the boys could keep their father, and that once this book ends, I will have erased from your imagination all future winters of the heart.

Cuddebackville is a tiny, rural hamlet one and a half hours northwest of New York City; population, a little over two thousand. Neither my husband nor I had heard of it when I saw the classified ad in the Times. Although he would have been content to stay where he was, in a huge Victorian twenty minutes outside the city, he came to agree Cuddebackville was where we belonged. The Cuddebackville house had been an emu farm, and was located at the top of a mountain on twenty wooded acres. As Jon said, we had twenty acres, but not one of them was level. After we had been there a week, I said, we didn't buy a house, we bought a boy scout camp. It was the only residence on a back country lane called Horseshoe Bend. In addition to the main house, there was a barn, an aviary, emu and llama pens, and many outbuildings, which gave it the appearance of a quaint village, a river, and a guest cottage – or what our British neighbor called, a Wendy house. We put guests in the cottage, golden pheasants in the aviary, adopted two dogs from the ASPCA, merged our three cats, and put goldfish and bullfrogs in the garden pond. When I woke up there mornings, it was as if the world was entirely made up of tiny gaping mouths needing to be fed. Anyhow, we immediately set about trying to fill the house with children. Jon had been a widower for thirteen years and reared two little girls alone. A month after we began dating, he signed a contract to write a biography of the pope, John Paul II. It would be his eighth and final book, and a sweeping departure from what he typically wrote about: the mafia, the meat market, the CIA, bank scandals, crooks, murderers, covert operations, devious businessmen and evil politicians. At his memorial service a former colleague at the Wall Street Journal where Jon had been a front page reporter for nearly two decades, recalled how Jon said he always wanted to write a front page story calling it: There Are Many Bad Men In The World And These are Them, and then just listing the names. He wanted to save the world through journalism and believed one person could make a difference. That's why he took on the pope, a man who by the end of Jon's writing, he would respect and love nearly as much as his own father. Just as he attempted to turn a man into a book, I arrange these facts out of unsensory words, all pointing to someone, but lacking the exquisite possession of his presence.

By the time you get to the hospital, your husband is disoriented, between the bleeding, the drugs, and the fear. He has lost all feeling on his right side, which seems a major loss since he was right-handed, but little do you know how much will finally be lost. If it were only a matter of having to relearn how to dial a phone or lift a fork to one's lips and stop playing tennis. The ancient Greeks used to give a full synopsis of their plays before the performance, so everybody knew how they ended. Hitchcock stressed suspense over surprise. But this is not a horror movie, though it still seems like it; it is not the type of tragedy that allows the stricken actor to shake out his right leg and go home for supper. Of all the lost boys, it was only Peter Pan who could not distinguish make-believe from true life. When the doctor finally enters the room, you quickly find him dreadful, perfectly dreadful. But apparently he is so upset by the prognosis, he doesn't know what to do, so he avoids looking at you and only vaguely addresses your questions. Eventually you make an excuse and leave the room to speak to him privately. You say it will be impossible to work with him if he doesn't communicate any better. He says he had hoped you could read between the lines. At some point Jon notices the two of you talking and becomes agitated, insisting he know everything that is going on. You return to the room to console him like a walking film of a building in perpetual demolition, and in the ugly room your heart breaks and breaks, but secretly behind your smile that says everything will be all right, and quietly, inside the hand that holds his. Shortly after, the nurses make an excuse and send you away. In the hall, one says the doctor wants to speak to you and she leads you down a long, beige hall and another long, beige hall, and another and another until you know with absolute certainty: you are lost. The room smells of hamburgers and onions – someone's just eaten their lunch. You are sick. And then the doctor arrives and just comes out with it: your husband has three months to live. Three weeks ago you had a baby; almost three months ago you met the pope; there are four of you now; you are completing your fifth year of marriage; how can a whole human being, a husband, a father, simply be gone in three months.

Most days my mother or father or stepdaughter or sister or one from a small army of friends would watch the children in the hospital lobby while I would be upstairs with Jon in his room. Even a few of my aging, bachelor poet friends would babysit, mentors I met in my twenties and spent hours with discussing art and poetry in downtown bars like the Lion's Head. When the baby would start to cry, usually because he was hungry, someone would phone the room. Because the elevators were so slow, by the time I got downstairs, Peter would be wailing. But I would quickly tuck him under my shirt, and he would latch on with a sublime greed for me, a complete abandon of distraction. With him then settled and happy, there suddenly would be a comma in the interminable sentence, a pause in the nightmare that reminded me life was wonderful and love was everything. Everything. One particularly awful day, after two weeks of this, the older boy, then eighteen months, made a small commotion while I was speaking on the hospital phone to Jon. One of the receptionists came over to me and said I must do something about my children, that they disturbed some of the other families. Memorial Sloan-Kettering's lobby is a concentration of pure anxiety. You have to go out of its doors to get any perspective. It is not like a funeral home where death is resolved and has come and gone. It is death constantly in the making. There was a hideous trend at the time where men shaved their heads; the fashionistas and the cancer victims blurred as your husband's life was struggling to define itself (after, when I attempted to wear widow blacks because any other color seemed too vulgar a response, I hopelessly blended in with everybody else in the city; instead of mourning my husband, I could have been going to Soho). I called the hospital Planet Cancer. It wasn't gravity that held us down there, it was love in spite of everything else, and the constant dread of loss. Inside the rooms, barely stirring on the beds because of their pain and their fear, was a different beauty, suspended, crystallized, thinning as each day passed. You at first listen to her and tell your child to quiet down. But then you notice how small he is, and he carries that bottle around, and has blue eyes like his father. As she returns to her desk, you think he should be outside playing, but his mother must be here because his father is and so is his little brother and his half sister, and his grandparents, and everybody else we care about, he must be here because we are a family and we have always been together. And suddenly your rage erupts and you are a volcano and you walk over to this monstrous woman and say your child is marvelous, how dare you, he is part of a family as well, and your head spins as your voice gets louder and louder and it is really enough, really enough and you sit down and everybody tries to calm you down, a pregnant woman sits next to you in solidarity. But now another employee wants to speak to you. You have heard about her type; they get sensitivity-training because they are insensitive and she attempts to sit down with her false, ugly smile and you say please, and you beg her to stop smiling because you know it is not real, you are sure it is not, and you ask her to stop acting sensitive because it is so insensitive, and this very act is heartless. Must I nurse so much? is what she wants to know. I must, I must, I am afraid I fucking must, I scream.

It is your forty-first birthday. You are in an open-air restaurant in South Beach, Miami. You are five months pregnant with your second child. You, Jon, your son Woody, who just celebrated his first birthday four days before, and your husband's friend Dirk, another journalist, are all eating spaghetti. The ocean is across the street. The evening is balmy. With no wall between you and the street you can watch everybody pass. The quantity of temporal beauty is staggering, a parade of barely dressed men and women in citrus-colored garments, all embodying only the most desirable attributes in the extreme: very white teeth, very long legs, very bronzed skin, very shiny hair. They are so beautiful they could almost convince you the cigarettes they puff, the alcohol they drink, and the drugs they take, won't lead to meetings in church basements or kill prematurely, but continue to bring endless pleasure. Latin music pours from the open air bars out into the streets and all the beautiful hips swish and sway. That night it felt like the whole world was happy. After dinner you say good night to Dirk who will soon learn his wife is pregnant, and you and your husband take Woody to see the ocean, defined only by the light falling from the moon and stars, and by the sound of the waves. Suddenly the music finds you and you put the baby down and each of you take one of his warm little hands and in a circle, you dance, the baby shaking his hips as the three of you laugh and spin. In nine months the man dancing will be gone, replaced with a statue in a box whose marble face you kiss a last time. A year after that you learn Dirk and his wife had their baby and then he too was gone, his death resulting from brain cancer. And people will pass their graves just seeing carved stones and mowed grass, the shells from South Beach I collected that next morning and arranged at the base of the grave like flowers might be curious to them, but mean nothing, for no one will know how happy these men were just the other day, how beautiful they were, how long they could laugh and talk, how joyfully they could dance and make love. The stones aren't stones, but mirrors we cover our eyes to see.

We live on a quiet street of modest houses, mature trees, and sidewalks that seem to lead everywhere for small children on training-wheel bikes. It is especially quiet at 6:30 a.m. in late May in such neighborhoods. Yesterday morning I awakened before the children. I made coffee and brought my laptop downstairs and sat on the sofa waiting for it to start up. Waiting for its artificial dawn, its lack of silence, its arrows pointing up or down but never to heaven and never to hell, to pull words not out of the metaphorical darkness of ink or the humbler lead, but to state my miniature universe out of the arrogant works of technology, out of light, a light as if to mock all gods, as if to deny the existence of people who still go to rivers to bathe and collect water, who make their way entirely from a pattern of stars. Here, instead of wilderness, a wilderness of time, a bewilderness. A blank screen is not a blank page, but my mind — absolutely blank — darts around the room: backhoe, fire truck, apatosaurus, tank engine, pictures of the four of us, like icons bordering the blank screen. Blank, blank, blank. But not the type of blanks Emily Dickinson wrote about. Not the type of blanks defined by a constellation of words. This is the blank that took the place of a man. Now suddenly a word: "Mom!" from the second floor. And there it is, a word I had indirectly made, tumbling out of heaven and down the stairs like a rubber ball, followed by the three year old boy with blond curls who had just uttered it. Woody ran to my lap, followed by two-year-old Peter with a sleepy grin. I put aside the computer, trumping Shakespeare: my two boys beat his kings. We are the Kwitnys and there are only three of us who live on Wilton Street.

When you are driving say, it may be the sight of a forsythia cascading down a stone wall that reminds you of the country house and then you watch him collapse again, rise up to whisper in your ear, I need you; you see the bedsore, hear the scream as a catheter is being administered, then see his fingers start to blacken signaling the last breaths. You won't be able to recall if you kissed him the last time your eyes locked, knowing this time probably was the last. He sang the hymn, How Can I Keep From Singing, before they wheeled him into the operating room to remove the main site tumor, and then kissed you deeply from the gurney, even though you had a cold and his immune system was depleted. The song ends, All things are mine since I am loved; it is what his grave now says. Because you carry these things, your eyes can't help but betray how much sadness you have at hand. But my eyes also carry the memory of him singing, of his face at the sight of our children being born, when he asked me to marry him, the way he smiled the whole day when we did, how he looked when he mindlessly stepped into Rome traffic so elated after meeting the pope, that I had to yell his name to stop him, teasing him that we had been blessed, not made immortal.

When your husband dies, his face becomes yours. Anyone looking for him finds you, an inferior him. The assumption – or is it, distraction – is that his completed life is also yours. You are a couple in spite of death, like attached twins, even though one of you cannot be seen or heard. If you are this new weird human concoction, then you can be explained: a misfortune such as yours only happens to other people and your metamorphosis points to another type of person. That is, because you have endured this loss, you must be more evolved (it is impossible to imagine how it gets broken down into hours and minutes and even seconds of tiny miracles and minute traces of hope.) You get a patina of spirituality you haven't earned, for you just stood there horrified as anyone would be. You grieve not as a saint, but as a wife, hating the attention of this new identity. Compassion and pity flood the streets of you. You are now an object of fascination. Compassion you can bear because it is not exclusive. Pity, however, is dreadful. Not looked at, but down to. But you are not a sorry creature, tragedy has not replaced happiness: it hangs next to it, like a companion mask. It is in every room you enter and it waits to leave with you when you depart. Not even the children can divert attention from it. If they are happy, everyone thinks of the missing father; if they are sad or cranky, the mind wonders if only he were here now. You want to say, but this is the way normal children behave. As for you, when the grace they have projected upon you, slips, because you were hundreds of other things before you were a widow, it becomes very confusing. Yet, no matter how much they call you widow, no matter how many sad things you have seen, you are not a sad figure.

Jon had lost all feeling on his right side from the stroke, but by the end of September he could get around rather well with the walker, and had even taken independent steps around the apartment. He dressed in a suit for the meeting with his doctor, wanting to show the doctor that he was still a man, that he was worth saving. Peter, now two months old, came with us, strapped to the front of me in a baby carrier, his little head resting on my chest. The doctor mentioned he had just returned from his vacation on Martha's Vineyard, but it sounded like he had said something obscene. How effortlessly he must have twirled the ice in his drink and gone out to the porch to appreciate the view of the sea, as the other man dealt with moving the mountains of his legs with the Hudson River brownly dragging a tankard. But a gift: Jon's main site tumor was practically resolved. He might have gained a year to live. We left a bit drunk on the news: a year instead of a couple months. A year instead of old age. As we were just about to make our turn onto Riverside Drive, a policeman was making routine stops. Apparently my jeep had been due for an inspection nine months before. It was an oversight that should have cost a few hundred dollars. He had taken my driver's license and car registration, and seemed to betaking forever. I had been away from Woody for hours and Peter needed to be fed. I suddenly jumped out of the car, the empty baby carrier flapping here and there as I stomped over to the officer. I said is this going to take much longer? I've got a toddler who hasn't seen me all day, the baby who needs to be nursed, and I've just been told if we're lucky, my husband has a year to live. In the thick, unhandsome face, I watched the human heart race through the eyes and brows and down the furrows to his mouth where his bottom lip dropped to reclaim this man from a position, like the doctor's, that in attempting to perfect failings, more often turned away. He could say nothing but that he would be right there. My Alice head still spinning in its Unwonderfuland, I marched back to the car, mother bear, wife lion, panting. Jon said I can't believe you just did that. In seconds the policeman returned and asked me to please get the car inspected when I could. No ticket, no fine. He just wished us good luck.

How do I write the empty rooms? The echo my shoes made as I walked through endless vacant apartments straining to imagine a future. I would fix furniture here and there, unwilling to give up the dining room table, not out of a bourgeois need, but because it held nearly five years of our conversations, it is where our friends sat. Beyond the need for enough space for the four of us, I insisted on an apartment with dignity, and one with a river, a view of the water for Jon. It was how we decided on the country house: a mountain for me this time, water for Jon next. What makes us assume we will always have enough time, that no matter how small our spaces, there is enough room to quarrel, when the most any of us get is but a tiny cup of life, a droplet. Earth is billions of years old, the dinosaurs were here for millions of years, millions of years ago, Homer was born in 850 b.c., Christ is now two thousand years old, Jon lived fifty seven, we were together six. Human eyes are worlds about the size of marbles, but all of us act as if we are the sun, the moon, and all of the rest the stars, able to challenge, deny or play God. When Jon was markedly improving in September we would look at places together. We drove to Jersey City, to a new complex of luxury apartments on the water – Jersey City meant it was affordable; "new" meant that it was likely wheelchair accessible; "luxury" meant there might be enough space with a washer and dryer on the same floor as the apartment. The apartment itself was bright and ample, with a breathtaking view of lower Manhattan. We sat on the promenade and drank iced coffees, neither of us mentioning the idea that we were a Holland's Tunnel away from the city – the hospital – and put one thousand dollars down. For weeks following, I tried not to erase the warmth of that day. Instead, all I could see was the loneliness of winter if Jon didn't survive.

I wish I could tell you with the coming of the daffodils, that Jon's tumors were resolved, that the boys could keep their father, the girls their mother, and that once this book ends, I will have erased from your imagination, all future winters of the heart.

What about the other daughter, the one who couldn't say goodbye; the one I mention because she belonged, and leave unnamed because she was lost. Not to death, but to him, because people do get lost. If this wasn't a true story I could make her fit here. I wish I could somehow put the two together with those first yellow flowers bunched in her hand and paint the sky a blue we all agreed upon. But because the way he loved her was misunderstood, because he became so strange to her, because he loved her and she loved her mother, and she couldn't say goodbye, I shall have to leave the rest of this page the way I found it.

The week before he died we stood in an empty living room on the Upper West Side considering another apartment. He wanted to know what I would do with the windows, what kind of curtains. It was unusual for him to care about such things. Yet when well-intended friends had called him at the hospital to talk about sports, a favorite subject of his since childhood, he said he feigned the old interest out of respect, but all in all, there seemed little point to it now. Being on the boundary between life and death, as the pope called it, when he spoke to us on the thirteenth anniversary of his assassination attempt. We had no idea that in two months, a month after Peter's birth, Jon would begin to fall across that line forever. The windows of this empty living room might frame everything we meant to each other. Perhaps he was thinking about that. Or perhaps he wanted to meet me more than half way and show an interest in something I enjoyed. His home was important to him. Unlike the apartment where we stayed on Riverside Drive, this one didn't have a view of the river. I wanted Jon to have a view, but I was also haunted by the idea that our Riverside Drive apartment would be our last place together because of it, as if life was fair enough and made sure, before taking Jon, he would finish his book, have his sons, meet the pope, and live on the water. But unlike the other apartments I'd seen in the city which were cramped and dark and featureless, this place had a pleasant light, original molding, glazed tiles in the bathroom, wood floors, a refinished kitchen, and it had a dining room. Maybe this was the charm that would stave off death. He stood, leaning on his walker, so ill, having just had surgery. They wouldn't rent us the apartment unless he saw it. Leaning on that walker, so ill, in the middle of an empty living room, the real estate agent looking helplessly on as Jon and I longed for a list of banal problems: starting with, what shall we hang on the windows? I could have made hundreds of other decisions. I could have married someone else. Except for his death, which I'll never understand, it otherwise all seems right. The places, the people. It is hard to imagine it. A leaning tower of seconds. I write to the soft snoring of my children sleeping in the next room. The rooms are not empty. On the contrary, I have rather crammed us into a small duplex in Princeton and painted the rooms the colors of flowers, and have done numerous things with the windows. He never would have agreed on this place. It would have been too small for us, but it also wouldn't have had the stature to hold him. And though he loved bright colors, I wonder what he would have thought about the pink I painted the bedroom. A male friend called my house overwhelmingly feminine. That word, at first charming, soon pointed to Jon's absence: the absent presence, as the earth artist Robert Smithson called it, such as the holes rocks leave when you pull them away. If Jon were here, our bedroom would not be pink, it would be a compromise. The last suit of his I couldn't bear to part with, hangs in the closet; the tie he wore to meet the pope, is rolled up in a shadowbox; the trunk beneath the television is filled with his things; each a stone making a path back to a man who once lived, who I loved so much.

Without him, there is too much of me. I write him into this morning, into my children's days and nights. I repair the past by imagining him coming home from work to play ball with the boys. How much would we have twisted into turmoil without the cancer to show us how much we loved and valued each other? The second anniversary without him passed. Few besides me remembered, but why should they, life is greedy, we have to work hard to keep the dead alive. Queen Noor said it of her king, a king! whose memory she works daily to keep alive. A list of war veterans on a plaque outside the local firehouse reads: Lest we forget. The plaque of names of men who not only died in some brutal way, but also laughed, made love, read a newspaper, regretted what they said, and who were once little children that amused adults. Since the past can so easily drag us around, a forgiving heart frees the soul, and mostly the mind. If Jon had survived, I would have been his Zen wife, mellow as a scented candle. Without cancer, we would have roared for personal time and an equal division of labor. Without him is like living with a whole side of the house gone. It is impossible to list what you lose when all of him is gone. I sometimes long for an island of widows and widowers with little children, who would recognize my face, who would scream at night to the sky for the reasons I do.

Jon wouldn't have written this. When it was suggested to him at the hospital he write about his disease, he just shook his head and said there are so many other things to write about, why be defined by cancer. He was more interested in people who made deliberate choices about their fates, whether they would be good, such as the pope; or evil, like the mafia, the bank swindlers, and other bad guys he mostly had written about. But I now have an assumed identity, a marginal one like a color on my skin people distrust and I can't for the life of me fit the way I once did in the world. As much as I hate being a widow, I repeat to myself: I am nobody, I am nobody, I am.

Today I took the children to the park where the four of us with Susanna, had once gone for a Sunday picnic. Jon is perpetually lying on his side on a blanket, propped on an elbow, under a particular tree, reading. Peter was a week old. Now the children run back and forth under that tree, recklessly through his image, reinforcing it over and over again. Reading the local paper, I notice an ad for the house we had subleased for two months before Jon got sick. The owner is off to Vermont, from May to October, and wishes to let it to a "responsible couple." Obviously he is done with children and would rather say, a responsible couple that promises not to die from May to October. He was livid that we broke our lease. I haven't seen the house since I returned. It's the beginning of my past. My friend Nancy offered to pack it up because we were already in the city. As she walked through the rooms, I described over the phone the things that were ours. It was a beastly hot August day. When she had finished loading up the car, the car alarm went off. But because it was Jon's car and a foreign car, she didn't know how to disengage it. She called an Alfa Romero mechanic and he tried to talk her through the problem. But the alarm blared so loudly, she had to run with her cell phone out to the street, get the instructions,then run back to the car to try to fix it. After an unsuccessful hour or so, completely exasperated, she said she would pay anything if he would come out and help her. I don't recall when she told him our story, but after he fixed it, he refused to take any money, and only wished us the best. After Jon died, I asked that instead of flowers, donations be sent to cancer research. When I went alone into the funeral home to say my final goodbye to him, there was one bouquet of flowers, with a note from the doctor who delivered Woody. A whole room full of flowers would have been too much. But to be alone with my husband and those flowers, was like standing with Jon on the mountain and looking at the field after a snowfall, with the peace to note every detail, a passing bird belonging for a moment. Our family and friends couldn't have been kinder or helped us more. As for the complete strangers such as the car mechanic, the policeman, and the real estate agent, they accompanied us so briefly, sharing their beauty like a passing bird.

A private swim club in Princeton. Families wearing the minimal yardage of lycra to suggest they are not mostly naked, yet speaking to each other as if they are fully clothed. I am always embarrassed. Especially now, because a black bathing suit makes me less invisible – or less visible, revealing down to the most minute details, my nakedness, my lack of even flesh. My body, without the man who once loved and desired it, moves in broad daylight like a nocturnal animal that has confused the hour. As an artist's model, I once posed nude for at least an hour; it was when I had to walk unrobed across the room that I became naked. Among the ark of couples, I attempt to look normal, to wrap a towel around myself when I walk the entire length of the pool to get ice cream for the kids. We had just returned from a three week stay in the Midwest, rushing out because Jon's mother had gotten pneumonia and wasn't expected to survive. But she did and the boys climbed upon her fragile lap and Woody asked, Why does that grandma sleep so much? Anyhow, I was tired and the boys, ever tireless. We were at the pool to meet my friend and a woman friend of hers I had never met. After introductions, I went to be with the children in the shallow end. My neighbors soon offered to watch them and I went back to the cluster of lounge chairs to talk. My friend's friend and I spoke easily and soon exchanged telephone numbers. When she saw my last name, she said she once knew a Kwitny who worked for the Wall Street Journal, was I related? My whole day changed and for a moment it felt as if I had my husband with me at the pool. She was in Nicaragua with Jon on a trip Abbie Hoffman had organized. She remembered Jon because he was the only journalist to speak out in a room full of liberal press. He challenged that the leftist political situation in Nicaragua was little more than a velvet glove revolution and that everyone, instead of just towing the accepted line, ought to be looking at it more honestly. She was in awe of him, and had gone to hear him speak over the years. At some point in our conversation I noticed Woody treading water. For my neighbors who were standing near him, he looked like any child swimming, but I knew he couldn't. I screamed his name and ran to pull him out. He was sobbing and scared as I wrapped him in a towel. The whole pool became still. I have been given everything: two healthy, beautiful children; my own health; six years with a man I loved; I don't have to worry about war, or not saying what I please, or whether my children will have enough for dinner today and drink clean water; I have as many choices as any person probably could, my list is endless, but at that moment, I had nothing if I didn't have my children. Absolutely nothing. My husband was not with me at the pool. I wanted to throw up my feelings, to stop making a man into a god. I held Woody as tightly as I could.

According to our vows, until death do we part, we no longer belong to each other. But he still feels like my husband, I buried him with his wedding ring and my picture facing his heart. His stone marker is at least a place to put my hand – my hand, ever reaching out for his phantom arm or shoulder or hand. The children have no idea what a cemetery is or that this is where their father is. A year later I attempt an affair, but only briefly. For a moment I felt the children and I had returned to our proper dimensions, that speaking to someone tall in the evening made me feel like a woman again. But I always trip on those sticky feelings; Alice longs for a world of playing cards and talking rabbits and pills that adjust the size of a universe to suit her taste. It soon became a secondary pain, such as when I pinch myself as a shot is being injected or a tooth drilled. The greater pain soon returned and no amount of distraction could rid me of it.

When I lifted Woody in the kitchen this evening, he was eye-level to the top of the refrigerator. Pointing to a photo of Jon and me, I said that's daddy. He said I want to go in there, I want to be with my dad, and he arched his body as if to climb into the photo. I carried him into the living room and said I would show him photos of him with his father. In my head I imagined a more recognizable Woody. Instead, there was only a bald-headed baby in Jon's arms, no older than a year and a half in any of the photos. It could have been any baby. Although I said, that's you with daddy at the pool or that's you and daddy in Italy, each image seemed to fly off the page. Unconvinced, he ran to play with his brother.

So many people carry around guilt when a spouse is lost. One woman I heard of recently had stopped sleeping with her forty-two year old husband because he snored. Then he died one night in his sleep. The morning Jon had the stroke, I told you we had just made love, but since I had just had Peter three weeks earlier, it wasn't something I wanted to do at all. In the shower beforehand, I was building up resentment, and almost said something to Jon, but I didn't. Instead, as both babies slept, we went outside, and then in an hour or so, it would all be over for us. The next four months was a dress rehearsal for death, no matter how much of a fight we gave it. Anyhow, this I bring up because in retrospect, I wish after that morning, there hadn't been any fights. I regret every one and although I can say my nerves were gone, exhaustion, postpartum hormonal changes, worry, fear most of all, and the idea that healthy people argue, dying ones don't: therefore, if we fight, Jon is okay and our lives are normal, it doesn't stop the pain that still resonates from those hurled, loud, poorly chosen words. It is easy to portray Jon as a perfect human being, to his sons, to my new friends in Princeton. But all of us who knew him know he wasn't, just as no one is. At his memorial service, a friend said of him as FDR had said of Anastasio Somoza: "He was a son of a bitch, but he was our son of bitch!" What I finally came to realize was that even though we were horribly imperfect, behaving badly at times for whatever reasons, we managed to perfect our love, and I mean that without a trace of the romantic. We learned to love each other truly. I have heard others tell of this. One woman's father said his wife had never been more beautiful than during the last months of her life. I long for Jon and the blissful oblivion we had that made us think we had forever to fight and make up. This gooey philosophizing, this ugly halo I got for just being a young widow with two little kids, is something I'd like to hurl like a frisbee. I am a monster human like everybody else, who longs for another monster human to make me human.

I walk around Princeton naked. If I am asked why I am here or what my husband does, it is like removing my blouse, my bra, then peeling back the skin across my breast, showing everybody my heart, then opening it and pulling it apart. If I keep my mind focused on all matters of the day, the minute to minute, about schools, face creams, quarterly estimated taxes, a parking ticket, a sled, a sale, new shoes for the boys, whether the table should be turned this way or that way, what is for dinner, bath time, bed time, story time, private time, if my mind is close to the ground processing all these worthwhile earthly endeavors, then I can forget for awhile that this really happened, that this is true life, that I have no idea where my husband really is. The least religious among my friends, joined the most religious people I know and prayed, lighted candles, or said masses for Jon in churches around the world. The pope's press secretary called from the Vatican to say he and the pope were praying for him. Our friends Walter and Jacqueline, a Jewish couple who just barely managed to flee Europe during the Holocaust, even went into a little church in Italy during their travels, to light a candle. A year and a half after my husband died, I became a Catholic. In the local Catholic church, a huge crucifix hangs with the head of the dead Christ slumped down on his chest. When death jerked the last breath away from my husband, that is how it left him. To the side of the crucifix stands a serene Joseph holding the infant Jesus. Between that statue of father and son, and the other of death and resurrection, I am braced. In there, I am convinced there is a soul left to pray for. The brightness of the day outside the church door blares even on the grayest days as the children rush out to make noise. A seesaw of banal, sublime: parking ticket, liturgy; tax law, I love you; shopping mall, terminal illness; what is it. As for me, I heard the last beat of my husband's heart. My ear clings to that darkness. Two new solar systems were discovered the other day making astronomers broaden their minds; a recently discovered piece of zircon in Australia, no thicker than a strand of hair, challenges the current wisdom of earth's age and what it was like in the beginning. Music has been scientifically discovered to be wired into every creature. Jon sang his life flows on in endless song. If only I could answer simply what it is we do, why we are here.

In order to survive as an animal you have to resemble a leaf, wrote a friend. Camouflage of the heart: attempt to look normal, act normal, wake up with the normal expectations of a day. Yet he is not intentionally bald and you have a closet full of clothes that belong to someone else. Almost two years later, you awaken at 6 a.m. in Princeton, but the rest of you is in the country house and both of you are crying. It began with you, exploding. A human building under demolition, books to be packed, furniture to be moved, dynamite blasting in your head, the world crumbling in your hands, how do you hide that? Where are the babies, Susanna, they must be there but that you cannot remember. The pain is what is so vivid. Was this before or after our fifth anniversary, the gift he had Susanna get and then he placed on our bed? The house gutted: all the chairs, beds, tables, and the sofa scooped up and taken away. But the paintings still hanged on the walls, with the family pictures and the books on the shelves. It was the center that was gone.

You walk one long beige hall after another, looking for certain elevators and certain signs. Although you cannot remember which pictures they chose to hang for this nightmare, you do recall the images did not belong. Replicas of paintings you viewed under different circumstances, their colors outraged by the hospital light, the incessant worry, the sudden endings no one is prepared for. Your husband is alone on a bed in a plain room, waiting to hear the final word from the radiologist. Your hands and lips lock with his like a door and that kiss will last forever. As you recall this now nearly two years later, in early morning as light slowly defines the trees and the birds sing out their existences, you have to force yourself to believe this really happened: you were once in a room at the end of a hundred false halls that led you only to the knowledge of your parting and the man on the bed you loved, who you promised to remain with until death, never imagining one night the second hand would suddenly stop for him and he would never know this morning or hear these birds. He would not be in this room last night when Peter, now a two year old boy with a darling smile, would not go to bed and propped himself up on the sofa to play with his mother's hair, and would lean over you after tossing the strands around and say, "pre?" meaning pretty and you hug and kiss your beautiful boy, and thank God he is happy and yours. Now the doctor has entered the room and unlike the reports he had given before, which had a trace of hope, he presents instead a whole barren planet of information: because your husband's main site tumor will not stop bleeding, and no surgeon will operate, they suggest further radiation. However, because your husband had received radiation in that spot nearly three decades earlier for Hodgkins Disease, and the body can only bear so much, they tell you it is likely your husband will be paralyzed within six months to a year. The disease roars up like a sea monster demanding all his manhood and I yell back it is not going to get it: Jon is more than his legs and I would rather have this man in broken parts than any other man. But the doctor isn't finished: your husband will unlikely live long enough to experience the loss of his legs. It is here Jon will not or cannot accept what he hears. It had only been two or so weeks before that the tumor started to bleed, that we were told the main site tumor was nearly resolved and that he might get a year, which he always imagined would be a lifetime. Cruel flower: he loses his life, he gains it back, loses his life. Black petals on a beige floor.

Black words, like paper lanterns, bob in the damp night air, tossing bits of light on the water. The best way out is through, said Frost. Black words, like scythes, cutting though this hideous picture to come upon a small blond boy barely two running through the halls of an apartment building with a soccer ball under each arm, proudly exclaiming, I got balls! I got balls!

You don't lose him once: you lose him daily. For widows without young children, there is no place to put all that love and that is why they seem so especially lost. In place of someone to sit with at the dinner table, to challenge or argue with, exchange a view or brush against as you move from one side of the room to another, there is only emptiness, silence, nothing. You don't even begin to remember him properly. You have to watch a video to hear the voice, the way he laughed. It was only two years ago but it feels like two hundred. A year ago the house was sold – a house I hated by the end because it was so difficult to sell and care for, but last night I watched it and remembered why we loved it, as it stood as the backdrop – with all the furniture intact and the lovely mess of living – of our family comedy: Woody a little over a year old hugging a chocolate Easter bunny to his chest, with Edgar our dog following him, Jon narrating and I providing the laughtrack. Occasionally he would focus the camera on me, lingering on my face or scan down my body, tenderly pausing. At first I wouldn't notice, and then I'd look up, and he would shift back to Woody. I felt adored last night, watching myself being watched by him.

Since Jon's death I have become wary – and weary – of similes. More than once, some wives,in an effort to be empathetic, have told me that because their husbands work so much, they are like widows. Like perhaps, but with the anticipation of return, the expectation–and from my own experience, the occasional frustration that would build when he was late. For one week, in Peter's third week, I was also like a widow, for Jon's new job required a lot of time. The first two weeks after Peter's birth, my mother helped, but the third week I was alone. I remember what it felt like at the end of the day, craning to hear the tires of his car crunch on the gravel, growing tense as the continuing silence outdoors converged with the crying babies inside. I wondered how I would have the energy to handle it, if it remained like this. And then it changed: it got worse. Saturday mornings come and the women who are like widows are out of the house, childless, and the dead-like dad is home, babysitting. Later that night, their children will unlikely say in a single breath: I'm firsty, I wanna watch TV, why did my dad die? A book came out shortly after Peter's birth called Do Not Erase Me. Taking the opposite course, I realized only by erasing myself, the way my huge, pregnant belly had erased my legs and feet when I looked down, would I be able to manage. When Jon got sick, if there had been more of me to make content, we all would have collapsed. Most of my adult life I had spent as a dreamer, attempting to vanish into greater identities, but now instead of just departing into a train of self-delusion, the features of my face blurred by the speed of such departures as I pulled away, I stepped forward, facing myself in the world's mirror, where people left blood drops along rows of corn, fell naked and nameless from the peaks of pyramids, descended into mines or factories, wrote poems in trenches before the final shot, were torn from families to be lead into rooms where they would never breathe again, were destroyed because they were female or male or twins or black or yellow or gay or sick or rebellious or old or deformed and so on until I multiplied into hundreds of Wendys: mother, wife, lover, friend, hunter, gatherer, miner, farmer, soldier, nurse, and so on, but not martyr. Having children and putting them before me had been the quantum leap, suddenly like adding windows to my claustrophobic being and breathing the sweetest air, as from oceans or deep countrysides; in giving my husband all of my heart, I found I was not the great person I had hoped to be one day, just simply greater than myself. Now I know what I am and what I was/I know the distance that runs from a man to the truth/I know the word the dead love best....I have lost it all and I have gained it all/And I ask for nothing not even/The share of life which is mine.

Before Jon got too frail and painful, I would climb on his hospital bed and curl up next to him and we would hold each other tightly. We never discussed what if the treatments failed and the miracles ran out and he should die. Never. We always faced it by editing out the parts we dreaded, and who knows, maybe something miraculous would happen. I would tell him about what Woody and Peter did over the week, then on weekends he would come down to the lobby in a wheelchair and get to hold Peter or let Woody squirm on hislap. He was touched by how Woody never acknowledged the presence of the wheelchair, but treated Jon just as he did when Jon was well. Sometimes friends would show up, and it would be like the weekends in Cuddebackville when we would fill up the guest cottage, but instead of drinking wine on the deck and looking at pine trees, it was this backdrop with these props. Maybe we were more alike than we or everybody else thought. Alike in our essential natures. We were hopeless optimists, used to miracles. On one of our first dates we learned that both of us felt the same about life support: we wanted to stay plugged into the world for as long as we could. This would come back in Jon's final days to haunt us. I stood at the foot of his bed as numerous doctors grew agitated trying to convince him that life support would be pointless. The truth was now a dull knife ripping and tearing apart the last scraps of hope. But it was I who had to sign the Do Not Resuscitate form. I called three priests before I did it and felt, despite my best efforts, I betrayed Jon. Truth and lies were practically interchangeable with death this close. Yet to have taken the hard practical look at our situation all along, if we consciously thought about it at all, would have only wasted what would be our brief time together. There was enough sorrow, there was no need to imagine more. During the hours of the morning before Jon had his stroke our only problem was how to attend a black-tie party with the children. The sun shifted its position a little more westward, and our concerns were completely different. For Zeno, his arrow would remain in perpetual flight as it went half the distance and half of that distance and so on. That mountain, which precipitant, has been collapsing forever, as the Baroque Spanish poet Gongora said. Even most of the doctors shied away from the language of the absolute. Give the measuring of time and its consequences to the neutral Swiss to make beautiful, but as for us, we preferred the flight, the mountain in constant flux, the uninterrupted embrace, and perhaps the inferior heroics of blatant denial.

The afternoon at first unfolded with nothing extraordinary to note: children on the front porch, the little girl down the street showing us her new school clothes, UPS delivering a package. There is nothing to indicate at first what the package might enclose. It is not until I dig deeply into the Styrofoam popcorn and pull out a small, heavy package that I realize I have in my hands my mother-in-law. Opening the cardboard box to find a pale pink urn I never realized this is how it would happen – send the ashes to me, I told Susanna who had experienced too much death in too short a time and no longer knew what to do. I am not used to the idea of ashes. Some family traditions are especially rigid, there seem to be only two in mine: we don't cremate and we insist on cornbread in our stuffing for holiday meals. I am still not used to death, it is just I have become fluent in its language. It had only been a little over a month since I had last seen my mother-in-law. She had the whole nursing home excited, organizing a small ice cream party for the children and sending the aides off for more cookies and juice. We sat in a common room with Musac playing in the background, practically blaring for most of the residents were hard of hearing. Four women made their way in wheelchairs toward where I sat with Peter on a couch. One slowly rose, bracing her large unsteady body on the arms of the wheelchair, then bent over to tickle Pete's chin. Mrs. Kwitny, in her nineties and barely alive, and since her only son's death, often struggling with dementia, cracked, Just what you love, old women who haven't put their teeth in. This is who I would slide under the antique tall boy in the front room, a piece of furniture that once belonged to her, as I recalled her lifting a hat from one of the ornate hooks and glancing in the mirror to apply lipstick. I knew I wanted her to be with Jon. About a month later, on a warm autumn day, I took the kids up to the country.

Margaret loads the trunk of my car with a spade and trowels, a tarp, and a package of crocus bulbs and we drive to the cemetery, which is just across the road. We take all the gardening implements to the grave with the box, which I have concealed in a bag and begin to dig a small hole. The boys are of course having a tremendous time of it, each gouging the earth with their own little shovel. Meanwhile the midday siren blasts, making me jump, as I am paranoid we will be caught grave digging, yet it seemed unnecessary to contact the funeral home for this, which seemed like a private affair. The urn doesn't require much of a hole. But just before Margaret puts it in, she drops it, for its heavier than it seems. The only message on the box indicating it might be precious is Fragile, Do Not Drop. But no harm is done, and it makes us laugh, and the boys make us laugh some more, and suddenly it feels like on this incredibly beautiful day with these wonderful people, in spite of what brings us here, that I have heard the great cosmic giggle — maybe God Himself laugh, and there is great comfort in that, that there is not only something beyond us, but that It might have a sense of humor. The box gets covered with smooth dirt and crocus bulbs. We top the hole with the grassy parts and no one could ever tell what we had just done. Susanna and I have a private moment at the grave while Margaret and Jerry take the boys down to the canal to throw stones in the water. People are walking on the other side, as Jon and I once did. In the void speed is like nothing else, it can caress the infinite, said the poet Jose Lezama Lima. Before leaving the cemetery, I brush off the stone next to Jon's. Jerry asked me why I did that. That's Jo's husband I say. Oh my, he says rubbing his chin. It happens, out of the most bizarre coincidence, to be the grave of my Princeton neighbor's husband. I lived at 15 Bank Street, she lived across the street at 16. Over coffee one morning, as I complained about the difficulties of trying to sell the country house, she naturally asked where it was. I said no one has ever heard of it, it's called Cudddebackville. She said why her husband had bought a winter cabin near some falls there. It turns out the house was down the mountain from my friend's house. Soon enough we learn both men are buried in the same cemetery. It took a few visits of hunting around for her husband's grave, to find that his was just next to Jon's, with only a couple unused plots between them. Another cheerful thought. Cuddebackville has only 2047 people now, Bank Street has only 13 parking spaces, both of us were in Princeton for no other compelling reason than we were not sure where else we should go and it seemed to be in the middle. As we drive from the cemetery, Susanna says it will be beautiful in the spring when the crocuses come up. We have dinner that night at our friends', Kate and Rob's geodesic dome, nestled in the woods. The next morning Rob takes the boys out to climb mulch piles and up on a digger and a tractor carcass. As I go out to look for them, walking toward the sawmill, I realize the woods smell like my marriage. I remember why I loved Cuddebackville. Like naming the family pet after a favorite author, you name your heart after it: Cuddebackville, and find that in the smell of pine on an Indian summer day with the sky as blue and crisp as one of your husband's dress shirts, that the four years it seemed you lost are now returned, intact as anything left entirely to memory. Without this sort of cosmic looking glass found in the landscape like a small lake held up to reveal parts you never even saw when he was alive, you might accept everything your mind tells you. It is him I miss, not the company of a man.

The morning after he died, I finally looked at his last request, which was in his computer. He wrote:

If you would grant me one favor, for the next while do not pray for anything. No requests at all, on my behalf or anyone else's. I have received such bounty over the past 57 years that to ask for more would be offensive. Of course I do want more, more of exactly what I've had and for as long as I can get it. I want to cover more stories, promote more justice, see Susanna continue to flower, and watch my sons grow up and flourish and do right as I know they will. But no fair-minded person could say I've been denied a thing. I'm the luckiest person I ever knew. I've claimed back 99 cents in change from every dollar I spent on life. I've trekked the bottom of the Grand Canyon and seen the sun rise from the top of the Hindu Kush. Another dawn, on Kilimanjaro, I circled the extra hour to scrawl my name at the true peak, a few feet above the false one. I never wanted to settle for second best. And I never have. Hell, I married Wendy Kwitny, didn't I? I've been accompanied through life by the best friends, had the best times, drunk the best whiskey, asked the most questions and tackled the biggest jobs I saw. I sought work I thought would leave the world and my fellow sojourners better thanI found them, as well as pleasure me, and am satisfied I accomplished both. I couldn't wish a better life on anyone than journalism. I couldn't wish a better life on anyone period.

1987–1997

Evening's Chair

As for this sea, no one can swim in it.
The beach is lost forever in the glass.
Although these words point tirelessly to your absence,
they are not a name shouted at the sky.
Because the Kobe widower cannot mend the ground,
he screams his wife's name to the sea.
At night, speaking to the glass of his perpetual bride,
he is not insane. For him, the window was torn in half.

As for me, I live in a modern city.
My ceiling is a sky blue umbrella.
My walls are newspaper and squares of light.
I am arranged like flowers in a still life.
Fingering the box of living, I gaze at a glass eye,
but I am asked no question. I string mirrors
like Christmas lights around my objects,
trapping the flitting seconds of my face.
On the floor, I force long sentences into picture frames.

I peer behind a lace curtain of cloud.
On the street, vague figures drop their hats,
vanish into invisible buildings of glass and rain.
Men bring me paper cones of flickering things
stained to look like long red roses,
but are black and crystalline by morning.
I wrap the smoke tighter around my weary body.
I am sorry, I have no reliable description for loss.
When I am sad, I fold myself up and put her neatly to bed.

Yet we are very loud about our feelings.
The man down the hall often sings like a suburban parakeet.
The woman upstairs fills a juice glass with tears.
I want to be very clear, but agony is the one whose sleeves
are soiled, and her child is also very dirty; it's a word we feel
is too helpless. Tragedy has too many cups; it sounds unreal.
As for love, I have heard that word, but I can't be more specific.
When I gave him my name, you see, he often said, Celeste.
It is like that here.

The Kobe widower cannot mend the ground.
The beach is lost forever in the glass.
As for this sea, no one can swim in it.
Although these words point tirelessly to your absence,
they are not a name shouted at the sky.
An empty chair faces the night.
How I long to fold my umbrella
and howl at the stars
until I no longer know why.

Gray Poem

Not that she knew gray better than the others,
although it lived between the houses
and under the trees.

Once she found it in another's eyes,
wandering, stooped,
like a half-starved dog.

Most knew it would not come undone.
In spite of this, she continued to work,
prying loose the darker parts.

Words clustered beyond her reach,
blankly touched her lips.
How often she failed, and hoped, and failed.

Why would the azalea blossom now?
She wondered, but the cat and its grayness
cared nothing for what she thought

and pitter-pattered away,
crouching for hours
behind a large, gray stone.

I imagine you have also wondered about the stars,
long before coming upon this gray ground
of diaphanous words and small flowers.

I merely point to the house
and the shadows that live beside it,
beneath the tree and all the objects

we usually disregard
until it rains, say,
and the lowly, invisible

umbrella suddenly rises from a hook,
and we are comforted
without giving it thought at all.

It is important that the moon appears here
among large animals,
such as the elephant with its gray enormous manner,

or with things whose importance
are often overlooked,
such as a hat tipped to say hello.

Are we really like the floating men in a Magritte
with their bowlers and mustaches
propped against a contrived blue sky,

endlessly falling
as we speak of another time,
and other matters, for instance,

whether it's better to spell gray
with an e or an a or like the French,
who prefer gris anyhow?

I wish, I wish I were a boat
and could sail to the country
of ungray things.

Looking Through Eyelashes, I

The cry of a rose
burdens the sky
and for days
it rains,

but the smallest bird
led us to sorrow.

It was too late, you see,
too wild for the cages of our hands.

My efforts to keep it dry,
to feather my heart,
made it more human
than it could possibly bear.

For three days we watched,
like weary gods
that had forgotten how to dance.

      Earth is too pragmatic;
only the sky pities the cry
of a rose

      or small bird
that seemed to be telling us,

see, the sky is falling,
it was only a cloud
that passed through your hands.

Looking Through Eyelashes, II

There are too many tears
in my rooms.

This morning
a residue of silence
fell on my arms.

The departure of a small bird
should have been meaningless.

They say there are too many birds
in the trees, my dear, turn

to a more important event,
the sky is the window's affair.

I lower my face,
but the rain is too much
and falls in my eyes.

Tin Landscape

Hills and trees roll toward me.
The sky rubs its face against my own.
Grass and stones run noisily across me
as if I were a bridge and they were drunk.
And the animals, tiny and vicious,
that scrounge about, digging in the spots
the sticky flowers missed.
I try to pull this landscape off my skin,
to seek out the roads with the speeding vehicles
and the faces watching from the windows,
but they don't see me. To them, I am strung together
with the rest of the poles, my arms sleeved
with pretty leaves, my cheeks as blue as the sky.
They don't know this sort of oblivion.
A tin boy, I rat-a-tat-tat my drum
and shriek.

This Way to the Egress
–P.T. Barnum

This table and chairs are not to be trusted.
I have had experience with furniture.
I have been sorely disappointed.
Take, for example, this bed,
this blue vase, these orange lace curtains.
Gravity seems to adore them.
But wait long enough, they evolve,
sprout a hat and coat, then up and leave.
They say it is me.
One more place mat and my life would be complete.
I have no use for magic; I can pull a rabbit out of the fact.
My room and its furnishings are a lie.
At the door, one line waits to enter, another waits to leave.
A mirror is attached to all I see, whomever I meet,
but the real picture will not be so contained.
Exiled to a wall without yellow paper, the hallways
to this cell stretch and stretch, each approaching step
I take, makes them longer. I have imagined her:
so frightened, so naked, so thin.
She does not eat the food that I eat,
and her marble knows no disturbance.
Her language is entirely vacant of words, but for one,
my name.

Refractions

You couldn't say what color –
as she moved past brown wall, yellow door,
a window full of gray, felt hats –
eyes that blue above blue sweaters.
She longed to show you why,
but as sun fell and broke into a hundred
shades of red, she turned away.
At night, she poured a cup of light,
nursing it like gin in the corner.
The color that was hers alone,
she would pull from a drawer.
No one would know that terrible stain
belonged to someone's eyes.
You kissed her against the sky,
among the violets and blue hydrangea,
crossing a sea of blue-green –
when you covered your eyes with her hair,
she thought it was time.
The color in the drawer, the one that love
made, was so dark and painful,
her hands trembled as she showed you.
You ran out the door, past the wall and a window
full of black, indifferent hats,
marrying the first girl you met
with eyes that stayed constant and gray
and never made you cry.
In your sleep, violets grow wild.

Verge of Silence

You are a fisherman,
just as the moon is a pearl,
as a poet writes
with a compass,
as I attempt nightly
to remove a necklace
from the water.
I've often dyed my dream
the hesitant blue
of your eyes,
and in the same breath,
reached for your arm.
On the verge of silence
your words
are like the small ship
that passes quietly
in the distance,
dividing the sea
from sky.

View

I am committed to this view.
I can rely on it.
It does not burden me with a change of mood
or stun me with invention.
Basically, the trees stay in place,
the squirrel flicks her tail,
the birds in the aviary jerk and crane.

Unlike much of what I do not see.
I noticed a man,
and paused at his elbow.

I am no longer the clever poet
who pulls a face from her hand.
My view stops at the squirrel,
the bird, the cage.

I make nothing spectacular
of the dog's bark,
and the words he wedged
like small pearls between the lines,
rolled off the page.

I look out the window.
Within an otherwise still scene,
a hundred Icaruses fall
like yellow leaves.

February 29

Of all the days,
you pick the least reliable.
What am I to do next year?
It will be too late.

I count without respite,
wanting to recall.
What spilled from my hand?
When did my irises turn blue?

Three years more and I will surely forget.
Soon, the yellow-headed bird
will be spinning around
the brown one.

A pregnant rabbit? Hah, my clock howls,
loud enough to break the clouds,
and so it rains,
rains in my head, on top of my

heart. Anxious for a sign,
I dip a knobby stem into a bowl
of warm ammonia, forcing the bud fists
to bristle with flowers.

I have seen too many
invisible things.
Missing days under the ivy,
in the chipmunk's hole.

No, no.
Something happened last year
I will say, crowning its blank
with a hat made of tin.

I stroke the fur of my words,
as if a hundred gaunt cats,
all bored, crouched, lording the steps,
eager for your return.

What They Recalled in Two Versions

An ordinary day
hovers over the carcass of a dog.
A woman lowers her sponge
and washes between her legs.
The men are on the rooftop
building a cage for the birds.
Children line the street
begging for food.
The old lady has dipped the same
tea bag three times today
and will do it again.
No one has sung a single word.
A few people have returned to smoking
and puff quietly in a back room.
In a back room quietly puffing
cigarettes are a few people
who have not spoken a single word
today. They will sing when the old lady
dips her tea bag for the third time
and the children feed the beggars
and a line forms on the street
to see the wages that the men got
for their building on the roof;
when the woman stops her bathing,
that incessant washing between
her legs, and what seemed perfectly
ordinary before, flaps off,
glancing back at the dog.

What They Recalled in a Later Version

The capture of the birds by the women
on the roof led a man to believe
he was not worthy of his children.
He would never sing a single word,
although he sat in a tub all day
soaping and rinsing. The top dog
drank tea in the afternoon
with the town queen. In a back room
nervously puffing on cigarettes,
they spoke incessantly
about the man who could not stop
washing. They were outraged. No one
begged in the streets and everybody
ate, so what is his problem? Many times
throughout the night one could hear
a few people cry out when the body
of a lion fell from the sky
and no one wanted to bury it.

What They Recalled in the Version That Was Written Down

Everyday in a beautiful little town
many birds of extraordinary colors
flapped about freely all day, to return at night
to the tall and handsome cages the town queen
had built for them with her own hands.
The small princesses quietly sipped tea
and nibbled iced cakes served to them by lions
that had been taught to speak. The young ladies
took the whole day to bathe and dress, then strolled
out into the evening where the young men
puffed cigars and formed long lines of poetry.
Everyone sang when night fell
and felt very safe, for on every street corner
a dalmatian the size of a house
stood guard, and quickly buried anything ugly
that fell from the sky.

When the Great Great Granddaughter of the Queen Became Enraged at the Final Version and Returned to the Town to Poke Around

The truth, explained the young town girl, was in an old cigar box
a beggar lady called Barbara had hidden in her attic.
Inside the box were five drawings signed in a large scrawl
by a young boy named Ernest, and a few fragments of tea-stained
notes, all anonymously written on light blue paper.
They had been hidden for centuries between layers
of pigeon feathers and smelled odd. Apparently the day
the men went up to the roof to build a cage for the birds,
a young woman named Dolores had been brutally raped by
a strange man who had come to the town to sell cigarettes.
He was never seen or heard from again. The whole town
believed the dog Homer had tried to stop him, for when they found
the dog, it had a piece of yellow plaid material between its teeth,
which was the same fabric of the stranger's jacket.
The whole town had been starving for days, you see,
and the only sound that could be heard was the sound of children
crying. And by the way, the young town girl said,
there was no so-called queen, then she shut the door.

What the Dog Saw and Never Revealed

It was an ordinary day and I was in the woods
With Dolores. She was the happiest I had ever seen her.
As I chased a rabbit down the path, I noticed a man
I had never seen before. As he walked toward Dolores,
his head was lowered and he was counting a thick wad of bills.
I decided to forget the rabbit and warn Dolores. I got to her
before the stranger, and barked and wagged,
but he was all of a sudden there, giving Dolores a big kiss,
and shooing me away. He showed her all the money he had made
selling cigarettes to the town people, who were so poor and hungry
their children begged in the streets. I could tell the guy was no good
by all the promises he made. And Dolores, who had gotten so skinny
and dizzy from not eating for the past week, believed them all.
She said, Homer, Go home! I pretended to obey and hid behind a tree.
Soon after, the stranger shoved Dolores to the ground, but gently
enough that even I thought for a few moments he might have loved
her. They started kissing and hugging, but then I realized
he was hurting her and that she was too overcome with fear
to scream. I ran over and bit the guy on the shoulder. That's the last
I ever saw. I heard a flock of birds flap off in the distance
and Dolores crying, Poor Homer.

The Bachelor Room

Every Tuesday afternoon Victor Zoar betrayed his wife and another woman he thought he loved, by meeting two women whom he did not love. Of these two, Soledad, was very beautiful and betrayed a husband; Rosa, the Cuban, was very common, but willing to do anything. She only met the man to be with the woman. Victor Zoar knew this but wouldn't dare let on, lest Soledad become appalled and not return. She, however, being the superior beauty, secretly adored her own importance in the room. Part of the year Victor Zoar lived in Mexico with his wife Alba, who spoke only Spanish and some insist, was truly blind. The rest of the time, he lived in Maine with a very blond, small-boned woman named Charlotte who spoke only English and whose vision was very good. He was from neither place, but from a country that existed only in his mind. In spite of being many husbands and many men, he remained a stranger. Because he never turned, he wrote elegantly toward identity, toward the states of birth, marriage and resurrection that followed quietly behind. He arrived at only words on maps. Women were like cities: their names easily replaced. Suddenly four breasts dangled before his eyes. Horrified, he could not place them. The faces and bodies to whom they belonged had fallen away. It was not the erotic experience he had come to expect from these afternoons. He longed to go home, but one was too close, and the other too far.

The Transient Bride

All of the furnishings in his small gray room seemed remote next to the great white shark on the floor: his bed. The painting, which could only be viewed from the bed; the walls of books spilling onto the rugs and growing into wobbly towers; a metal chair pushed into an enormous desk and all the writing instruments spread across it, in the glow of a desk lamp like zoo animals basking on rocks. A child's blanket floated in the center of the bed like a square island, leaving the edges of a faded green sheet to lap at its trim like a dry sea. The painting was of a stuffed animal, a dappled gray pony with amber eyes, crowded into a dark background. It looked real, and because of its shape, seemed to have been forced into the canvas rather than painted there. Because it was now a painting instead of a doll, this inanimate object suddenly seemed capable of moving; its glass eyes capable of seeing; and its inability to breathe, upon the verge of choking. It had what Auden called, a human position, embodying not rags to give it form and dimension, but the desire to rear up with the fury of a real horse. It stared at them as they animated the movements of their own captivity, the tripping desires and weak illusions they mistook for love. Everything was fine until she reached for a sock. They caught each others eyes and for at least a hundred seconds, dipped into the icy water of mutual self-consciousness. Her naked arms grew to the floor, legs multiplied, rows of breasts mounted her torso like an ancient fertility doll. Wings burst from his back and his feet turned into claws. The horse was too big for the picture. The blanket floated like a leaf on the bed. She wanted to bring everything to its proper dimensions, to fit inside that room, to be one of its belongings, but his bridge was no bigger than a shoe. She, a transient bride, knowing a thousand words for good-bye, left one and withdrew.

Four Winters

for Medrie MacPhee and Harold Crooks

1

A poem is normally not a candle holder.
Today I put in your hand
an object with an opening that might be a poem.
Don't be frightened: it merely looks like ice.
Feel how smooth, as if in the modern
language of this object, this language of Brancusi,
the ancient Cycladic art is reborn.
Its passion is private, yet a trace of it is betrayed,
as if caught unexpectedly in a photograph.
The air bubbles belong to someone from Finlandia.
In language, the lung is a small god.
For the centipede, amber is a sanctuary.
Here, a candle is not a candle.

2

Artaud perpetually writes himself into being,
toward his profile on a book, looking out
beyond the text, onto a world of burning candles.
His face is read, as if the eyes could bring forth
the miraculous birth. Here, the desire for life
and more life, breath and more breath,
transfixed like oxygen in glass;
oxygen in the blackened mirrors of his mind.
It is not this word that is so important, but the next.
I cup my mouth around an "I" like a glass blower
and pour as from a pitcher what I know of life.

3

Artaud said no one has ever written or painted
except to get out of hell. To conquer dryness, Van Gogh said.
Thirty-nine years later, out of a bedlam of fine lamps
and oriental rugs, I turn away from a world
that wants to shrink me, push me back into that jar
where my noises fit like everybody else's.
I have choked toward my rebirth, and choked again

at being grasped by your eyes. Lighting me
like a dry stick or candle, I am like ice in your hands.
In a place between day and night, I move my hand across paper
attempting
to hold and behold reality.

4

February 1947, Artaud writes: it is reality itself, the myth
of reality itself, mythical reality itself which is materializing.
Ten years later a child is born. Her wrinkled body unfolds
like a rose. Every part of her is interested in light.
She is an animal, untamed and unused to sharing space.
They put her in a glass jar, a vase, for she looks up
and with red hands, clenches fistfuls of air and eats.
She has no idea there was a Frenchman once, she would later meet
or a Dutchman who, sixty-eight years earlier,
would put on his head a hat made of candles and grin at the night.

To a Friend On the Occasion of His Fortieth Birthday

For Stef Kotsonis

If only the world were more tidy,
and I could reach out the window for a rose.

Open your hand.
Like the moon, I make use
of borrowed light.

Places are less generous than we think.
No leaning tower or narrow street
or row of palm trees
were ever sorry to see us go.

Note: the traveler takes a photograph or takes home
a souvenir, or takes with him the memory
of the local voice that twisted words so adorably,
the accidental love that took an hour to make.

Let us consider Freud,
who said the maternal body was the only place
a man could say with certainty
he had been there.

None of us arrive as men,
but as small ships
longing for the world.
All of us have our stories.
The sad ones usually crowding the rest.

Like these words,
in their black suits and unfashionable hats,
unreal as people in a photograph,
but use them or doubt them
or wipe your tears across them,
and suddenly they move and speak,
and offer a carnation of light.

Won't we all take something away of tonight?

You especially, who woke earlier today,
as you did forty years before,
with a cry – perhaps less terrified,
but no less real.

Look less for happiness, my friend,
and less for yourself among the odd things
that clutter the world. Pull out the wings
you were given that first breath
and dazzle us.

Flying around bedposts is for little children,
but soaring on a clear day
with the rest of humanity craning
their necks to decide what type
of bird you are,
is for the birdlike man,
who sings in spite of everything.

The Wendy House

There are no tears in the house of poetry.
                                    — Sappho

Gentlemen, the door is air.
Come in, the birds will adore you.
A house of words is not bricks,
but resonance. The roses are curious;
reading is a game of badminton
to them. Any English child has a name
for it, this place of pretend,
like the hat-crowned house the lost boys built
around the fallen Wendy.
There is only a noun up my sleeve.
It is true, too, an Arab child calls his verses houses
and may carry hundreds before the day is through.

Ladies, my frown returns like a homing pigeon.
My arm is paper, like my long brown hair.
I use my pen to chip away a whole,
crowd into this place where I am not alone.
Like Wendy, who wakened to mother lost boys,
I rub my eyes and teach lost words to fly.
I am sorry this chair is not wood.
That this cup is but two consonants, a vowel
and a syllable. Nevertheless,
I hope you are comfortable.
The roses say you are beautiful.
Today, the Arab children recite houses
to the English. Through the smallest windows,
Beethoven's laughter is heard.

Friends, the t is served. Please stay.
The sky is homemade and the birds are singing.

A Brief History

As you leaned to open the small iron gate,
a fistful of daffodils raised
like a torch, as if to pronounce to all days,
this was the first,

then you looked up and smiled at me.
I knew you already loved me,
as I hesitated on the step.

How ordinary those next five or six seconds
might have been, like the rest of time before I leapt

and made an entire life out of a single kiss.

Love Among the Cynics

He finally heard her say, I love you.
And as he marveled at the way
the words whirled through the air
like the plump little blue birds
in Disney movies,

every love poem
puffed up, turned green,
and stamped a foot.

Dancers collapsed, hiding their heads under tutus.
Monsieur, cocking an ear, burnt his pinkie in the toaster.
And Madame, looking up from her seam, pricked her forefinger.
A dog barked. A cat wailed. A mere goldfish
swallowed the moon.

Yonder, a field of poppies stood up on tippy-toes
and demanded in high-pitched voices:
BUT ARE YOU SURE THAT'S WHAT SHE MEANT?

One of the birds froze in midair.
A dancer poked her head out of lavender tulle.
Astonished, Madame lowered her finger from a ruby-smeared tooth.
The mere goldfish spat toward the stars.

His amore shot a gun toward the sky, startling
the poppies that flew away on red wings.

The moon threw a kiss.
I love you, too, he said.
The poems sighed and stepped aside.

Pregnant Pause

Men hand me their babies.
I only look like a mother, I tell them.

Soon I will put aside my name,
and wait among bird and animal sounds
for the new word to claim me.

My head brushes against the belly of a cloud.
My feet leave a message in the ground.
I carry a whole continent around my waist,

contrive a universe of small, blue things.
Miniature stars cluster around me.
Mother birds teach me to sing.

For a brief while, I am not lonely.
Wedged between my heart and soul like a book,
he sleeps to Vivaldi.

My body unfolds like an accordion
and I dance like a thousand stars
around the little boy

who lives in the moon.

True Love

Once I was the Queen of Hearts,
ruling small lands beneath my bed;
that was when the world was flat.
Gentlemen, no wonder you are sad.

Like a boat falling off the edge of the world,
that is how I found my voice.

Tiny dancer, twirling inside me,
I must learn to sing and play an instrument.

I write your name across the page
and watch it settle like a shadow.
Today, it points only to myself,
a borrowed ship sailing delicately
toward your first breath.

Joy rests inside my hand, I cry. You shift,
as I braid and untangle my sea green hair.

The Mountain
for Ulf Goebel

Regarding the trees, it was not that I forgot.
All that incessant pointing to the sky,
stars wincing in the branches.

Or the animals lingering near the fire,
their thin bodies so sad to watch.
We were all so hungry.

The animals are stronger now.
They listen to me, they lead me
quietly from the river.

The trees respond as trees should.
I kneel beneath them,
I close my eyes to pray.

You wonder why it is here I've come,
among these ordinary rocks,
and the damp, ruddy leaves,

on a mountain where no gods
made fire.
I shall say this much.

The birds, not burdened
with oracles, sit quietly
as old people talk.

The fruit have no metaphors to give,
and even the faintest stars show up.
Thin things break off

or are slowly drawn away.
Every word must weigh as much as rock.
The strongest light lingers for hours

in the trees. But more importantly,
it was the only place

besides the wind,

I could complete my sentences.
The elegance of this mountain
is how we move around it.

I shall pour in your bowl
a water made of stars and trees.
Give me some time.